CPS-MORRILL ES

3 24571 0902268 5   577 LAP
Decomposers

W9-ASR-768

DECOMPOSERS

Megan Lappi

www.av2books.com

AV² provides enriched content that supplements and complements this book. Weigl's AV² books strive to create inspired learning and engage young minds in a total learning experience.

Your AV² Media Enhanced books come alive with...

Audio
Listen to sections of the book read aloud.

Key Words
Study vocabulary, and complete a matching word activity.

Video
Watch informative video clips.

Quizzes
Test your knowledge.

Embedded Weblinks
Gain additional information for research.

Slide Show
View images and captions, and prepare a presentation.

Go to **www.av2books.com**, and enter this book's unique code.

BOOK CODE

U436141

AV² by Weigl brings you media enhanced books that support active learning.

Try This!
Complete activities and hands-on experiments.

... and much, much more!

Published by AV² by Weigl
350 5ᵗʰ Avenue, 59ᵗʰ Floor
New York, NY 10118
Website: www.av2books.com   www.weigl.com

Copyright ©2012 AV² by Weigl
All rights reserved. No part of this publication may be reproduced, stored in a retrieval system, or transmitted in any form or by any means, electronic, mechanical, photocopying, recording, or otherwise, without the prior written permission of the publisher.

Library of Congress Cataloging-in-Publication Data

Lappi, Megan.
 Decomposers / Megan Lappi.
   p. cm. -- (Food chains)
 ISBN 978-1-61690-712-9 (alk. paper) -- ISBN 978-1-61690-718-1 (alk. paper)
 1. Biodegradation--Juvenile literature. I. Title.
 QH530.5.L37 2011
 577'.16--dc22
                          2010050995

Printed in the United States of America in North Mankato, Minnesota
3 4 5 6 7 8 9 0 16 15 14 13 12

012012
WEP090112

Project Coordinator Aaron Carr
Art Director Terry Paulhus

Photo Credits
Every reasonable effort has been made to trace ownership and to obtain permission to reprint copyright material. The publishers would be pleased to have any errors or omissions brought to their attention so that they may be corrected in subsequent printings.

Weigl acknowledges Getty Images as its primary image supplier for this title.

Contents

Nature's Food Chain

All living things need food to survive. Food provides the **energy** that plants and animals need to grow and thrive.

Plants and animals do not rely on the same types of food to live. Plants make their own food. They use energy from the Sun and water from the soil. Some animals eat plants. Others eat animals that have already eaten plants. In this way, all living things are connected to each other. These connections form food chains.

A food chain is made up of **producers** and **consumers**. Plants are the main producers in a food chain. This is because they make energy. This energy can be used by the rest of the living things on Earth. The other living things are called consumers.

There are five types of consumers in a food chain. They are carnivores, decomposers, herbivores, omnivores, and parasites. All of the world's organisms belong to one of these groups in the food chain.

Some mushrooms are fully grown less than a day after they emerge from the ground.

Chain Reactions

If an animal's food source disappears, other animals will suffer and possibly die.

FOOD CHAIN

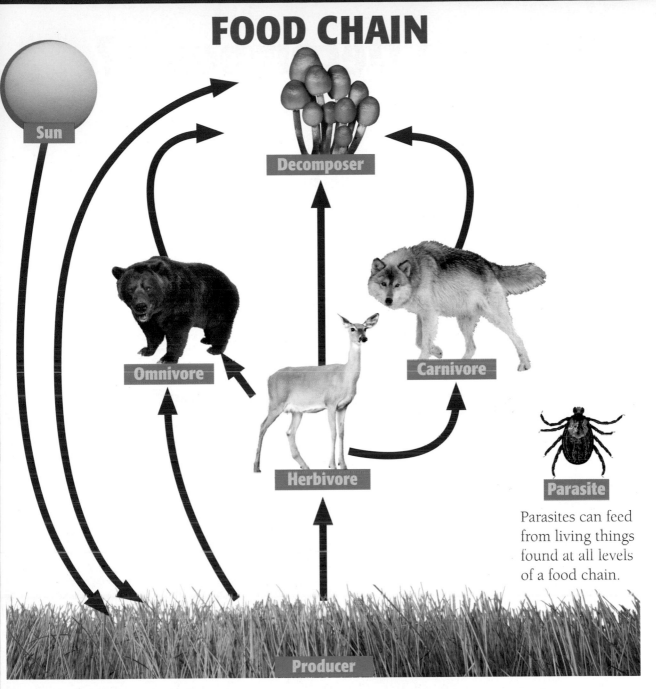

Sun

Decomposer

Omnivore

Carnivore

Herbivore

Parasite

Parasites can feed
from living things
found at all levels
of a food chain.

Producer

In this example, the Sun starts the food chain by providing energy for
grass to grow. The deer eats grass as its food, and the wolf eats the deer.
Bears may also eat grass or deer. Mushrooms receive energy from grass
and the waste left behind by wolves, deer, and bears. Parasites can be
found at any point along the food chain. They can live inside or on
producers and consumers. A tick can get the food it needs to survive
from a deer, a bear, or a wolf.

What Is a Decomposer?

Decomposers can be broken into two groups. They are decomposers and detritivores. Decomposers and detritivores are living things. They get their energy by eating and breaking down dead plants and animals. It takes many decomposers to break down decaying **matter**.

Decomposers help keep an ecosystem clean by clearing away the **detritus** left behind by plants and animals that have died. They are part of the **detritus food chain**. Decomposers are very small. They include tiny **bacteria** and **fungi**.

Bacteria adapt very well to the environment. They are found every place on Earth.

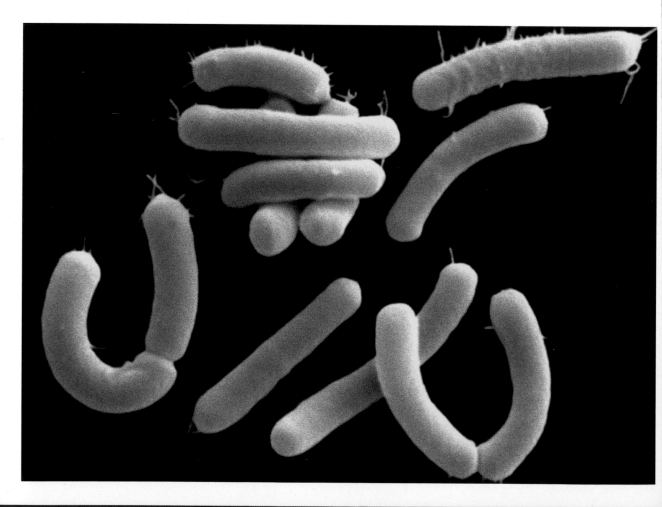

Animals that decompose dead plants and animals are called detritivores. They include earthworms, maggots, and termites.

Decomposers break down dead plants and animals using **enzymes**. The **nutrients** from this process pass into the air, soil, and water. Without decomposers, plants would not get the food they need to grow. As well, herbivores would not have plants to eat.

Some termites have special types of bacteria that live in their stomach. The bacteria help break down food into energy.

Making New Soil

Decomposers in a compost bin help turn leaves, twigs, grass, and leftover food into soil. Many decomposers, such as bacteria, are so small they cannot be seen by the human eye.

The Detritus Food Chain

Decomposers and detritivores are at the bottom of the food chain. They are very important because they eat **organic** material from dead plants and animals. They make this material into nutrients that help plants grow. This helps keep air and water clean.

Bacteria living in the ground add nutrients to soil. These nutrients are essential to the green plants that grow in that soil.

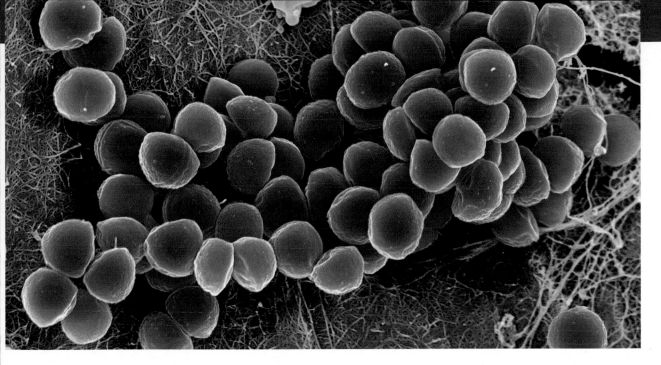

The process of breaking down matter begins with a detritivore, such as an earthworm. Earthworms break down detritus into smaller pieces. Then, tiny decomposers, such as bacteria, complete the process. They make the detritus pieces even smaller. Soil and water absorb these small pieces. This cycle is repeated.

Bacteria produce the enzymes needed to build up and break down organic matter.

The detritus food chain is made up of the following parts.

detritus + detritivores + decomposers = nutrients for air, soil, and water

Medical Helpers

Maggots are used by doctors to clean wounds. Maggots can grow about five times in size when cleaning wounds.

Billions of Bacteria

Bacteria are everywhere. They are so tiny that millions of them could live in a space as small as the end of a pencil.

Scientists once believed bacteria were animals because they moved around. Scientists soon realized bacteria are not animals. They wondered if bacteria could be **classified** as plants instead. Now, scientists know that bacteria are neither plants nor animals. They are a separate and distinct form of life.

About 100,000 individual bacteria can be found on 0.2 square inches (1 square centimeter) of human skin.

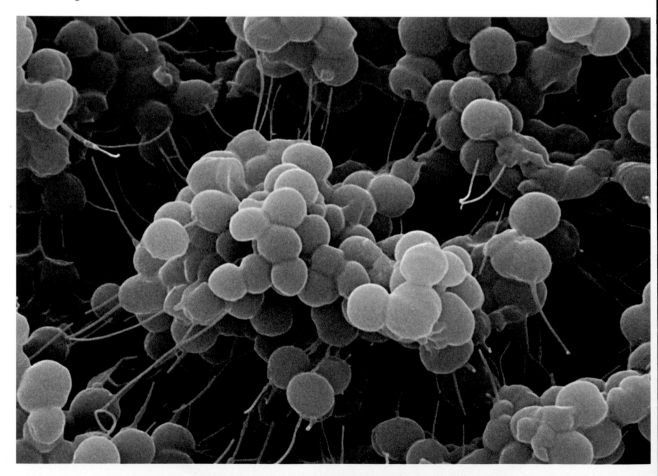

Bacteria that eat only dead plants and animals are decomposers. Bacteria make up the biggest group of decomposers.

Decomposers fill an important role. Dead matter and waste would pile up if bacteria did not exist. Bacteria help plants get the important nutrients they need to survive.

When a tree dies, fungi and other decomposers break down the dead organic material.

Heat Seekers

Some kinds of bacteria can live in very hot places. A type of bacteria called hyperthermofiles lives near volcano openings. Temperatures can rise to 212 °Fahrenheit (100 °Celsius) near these openings.

Freaky Fungi

Fungi are another type of decomposer. There are many different fungi. Some are very small. Others are huge, in some cases even as large as a dog. Most are not harmful, but a few are very dangerous.

Two types of fungi are white destroying angel and deathcap mushrooms. They are part of the *amanita* family. This is the deadliest group of fungi on the planet.

The only way to know which mushrooms are edible and which ones are poisonous is to learn to identify the different classes.

Some fungi are named after the foods they look like. For example, the "chicken of the woods" fungus looks similar to a big, yellow chicken. In Germany, people like to eat this fungus. Cooked chicken of the woods tastes much like chicken.

The umbrella-shaped form of a mushroom is the fruit of the fungus.

Potato Famine

In the 1840s, fungi attacked potatoes in Ireland and caused a **famine**. Many people left the country because they did not have enough to eat. Some traveled overseas. Many people of Irish **descent** still live in the United States.

Decomposer Close-ups

There are many kinds of decomposers. Some, such as bacteria, are so tiny that they cannot be seen by the human eye. Detritivores, which include earthworms and millipedes, are large enough for human eyes to see without a **microscope**. Decomposers can be found throughout the world. Some decomposers live in water. Many live on land.

Earthworms

+ can range in length from 1 inch (2.5 centimeters) to 12 feet (3.7 meters)
+ make tunnels in the soil that create space in which air and water can move around
+ waste from earthworms makes soil rich and fertile
+ when a plant dies, an earthworm drags it underground to eat it
+ some people put worms in their compost bins, even indoors

Ascomycotines

+ the largest group of fungi
+ found on dead animals, in fresh water, and in soil
+ yeast is an ascomycotine used for making beer and baking
+ ascomycotines are used make the **antibiotic** penicillin, which is used to treat infections

Mold

+ tiny plants from the fungi family
+ mold **spores** are always in the air
+ molds are used to make some cheeses and vitamins
+ mold grows best on soft fruits

Termites

+ groups number from 100 to 1 million
+ there are about 2,000 known **species**
+ most build their nests underground
+ sometimes known as white ants because of their color
+ mainly eat wood

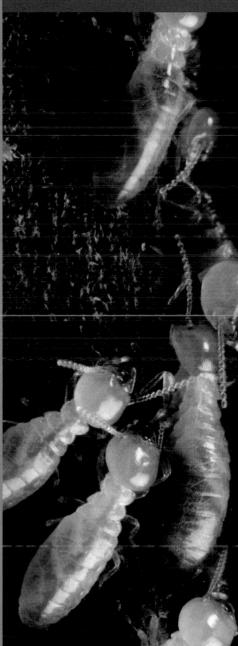

Maggots

+ look like tiny, white worms
+ **larvae** of the common house fly
+ breathe using two small holes at their back end
+ doctors use maggots to clean dead tissue from wounds

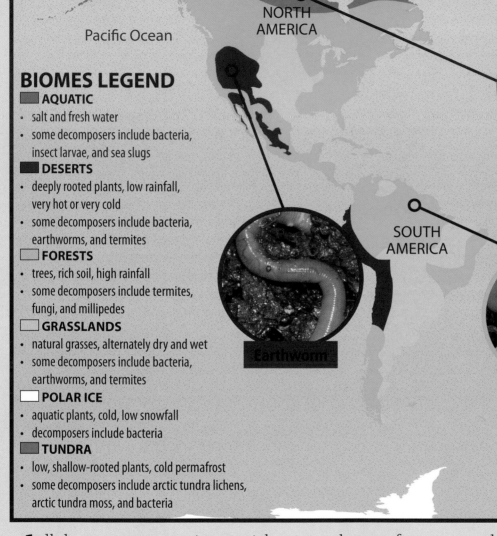

Where Decomposers Live

GREENLAND

Atlantic Ocean

Pacific Ocean

NORTH AMERICA

SOUTH AMERICA

BIOMES LEGEND
- ▮ **AQUATIC**
  - salt and fresh water
  - some decomposers include bacteria, insect larvae, and sea slugs
- ▮ **DESERTS**
  - deeply rooted plants, low rainfall, very hot or very cold
  - some decomposers include bacteria, earthworms, and termites
- ▢ **FORESTS**
  - trees, rich soil, high rainfall
  - some decomposers include termites, fungi, and millipedes
- ▢ **GRASSLANDS**
  - natural grasses, alternately dry and wet
  - some decomposers include bacteria, earthworms, and termites
- ☐ **POLAR ICE**
  - aquatic plants, cold, low snowfall
  - decomposers include bacteria
- ▮ **TUNDRA**
  - low, shallow-rooted plants, cold permafrost
  - some decomposers include arctic tundra lichens, arctic tundra moss, and bacteria

Arctic Tundra Moss

Earthworm

Millipede

All decomposers require special living conditions in order to thrive. The place where a living thing exists is called its habitat. Earth has many different **biomes** that serve as habitats. Biomes are defined by their climates and the plants and animals that live there. The world's largest biomes are aquatic, deserts, forests, grasslands, polar ice, and tundra.

A decomposer's habitat can be as big as a desert or a forest. It can also be as small as a tree branch or a pond. Each decomposer must live where it can get the food it needs to survive. Termites live in forests. They can find wood and other

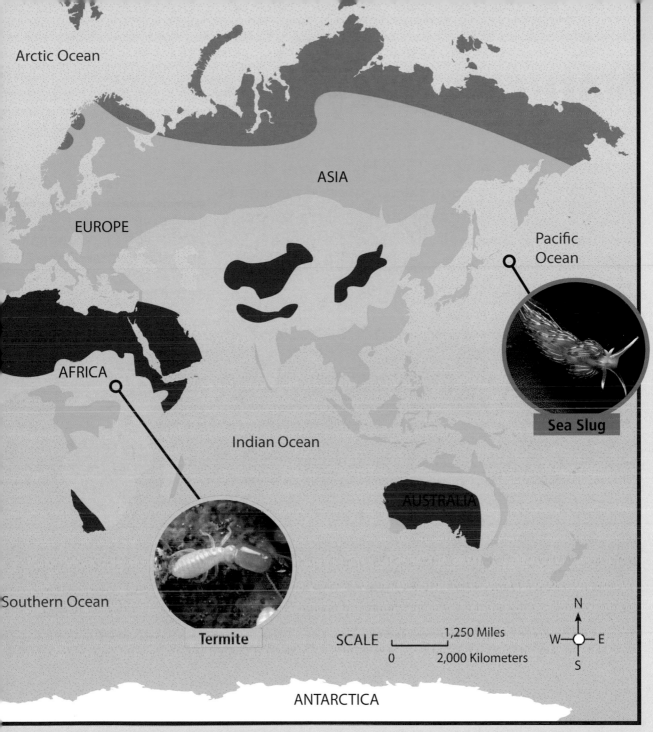

Arctic Ocean

ASIA

EUROPE

Pacific
Ocean

AFRICA

Sea Slug

Indian Ocean

AUSTRALIA

Southern Ocean

Termite

SCALE ⌐———⌐ 1,250 Miles
0   2,000 Kilometers

N
W—○—E
S

ANTARCTICA

plant material to eat. They would not live long in a polar ice biome.

A decomposer that lives in a biome in one part of the world might not live in the same biome in a different part of the world. For example, shitake mushrooms grow in forests in China and Japan but not in the forests of North America.

Look at the map to see where some types of decomposers may live. Can you think of other decomposers? Where on the map do they live?

Nature's Recyclers

Without the work of decomposers, the world would be a messy place. Imagine if you had to wade through dead leaves, logs, and other dead things every day on your way to school. If it were not for decomposers, everything that died on Earth would keep piling up. Lakes and rivers would be clogged with dead fish. Decomposers keep the world tidy.

There is more dead material, such as animals and plants, than living matter in bodies of water.

Decomposers also make sure nutrients from dead material are recycled back into the air, soil, and water. If there were no decomposers, the world would be very unpleasant. Nutrients would be trapped in the bodies of dead plants and animals. New plants would not be able to grow. Animals would have nothing to eat. Slowly, everything on Earth would die.

Water is necessary for decomposers to do their work. If an object does not contain water or is not exposed to water, it cannot decompose.

In The Field

MICROBIOLOGIST

Career
Microbiologists study microscopic organisms such as bacteria and some types of fungi. They study the ways in which these tiny organisms affect people, animals, and the environment.

Education
A bachelor's degree in chemistry or biology is required for most microbiologist jobs. For some more advanced jobs, a master's or doctorate degree is needed.

Working Conditions
Microbiologists work in many different fields. Some ensure food is safe to eat. Others study how bacteria and fungi affect the environment, while still others perform research in laboratories. Another job for microbiologists is teaching in colleges and universities.

Tools
collection jars, microscope, computer, test tubes, beakers, Bunsen burner, centrifuge, petri dishes, incubator

Oil Spill Cleaners

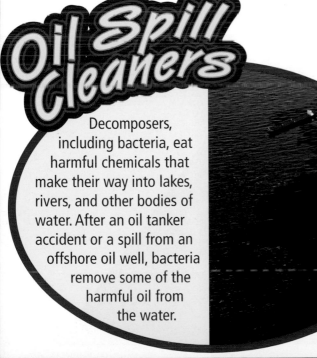

Decomposers, including bacteria, eat harmful chemicals that make their way into lakes, rivers, and other bodies of water. After an oil tanker accident or a spill from an offshore oil well, bacteria remove some of the harmful oil from the water.

Making an Energy Pyramid

A food chain is one way to chart the transfer of energy from one living thing to another. Another way to show how living things are connected is through an energy pyramid. In an energy pyramid for decomposers, one plant or animal provides energy for many detritivores and many decomposers at higher levels on the pyramid. When a plant or animal dies, it becomes detritus. Detritivores break down the detritus into smaller pieces. Decomposers break it down even more. Some of this tiny material returns to the soil, helping new plants to grow. In the example below, earthworms start to break down the jackrabbit, and bacteria finish breaking it down.

ENERGY PYRAMID

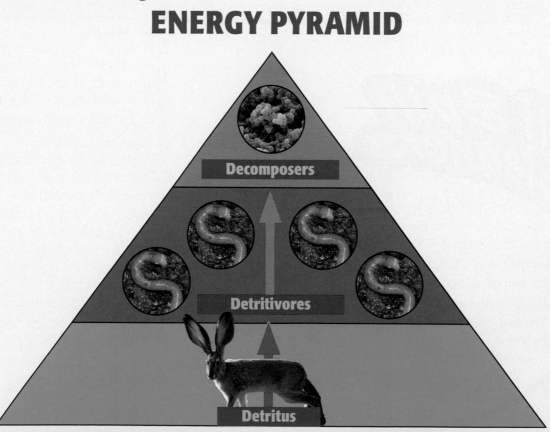

Decomposers

Detritivores

Detritus

Below are some examples of decomposers and the habitat where they live. Choose one of these living things and learn more about it. Using the Internet and your school library, find information about how the decomposer receives the energy it needs to live. Determine the plants and animals it uses for food. Using your decomposer, draw an energy pyramid showing the transfer of energy. Which plants and animals are a source of energy for the decomposer you picked? Do other decomposers receive energy by further breaking down detritus after your decomposer is done?

DECOMPOSERS

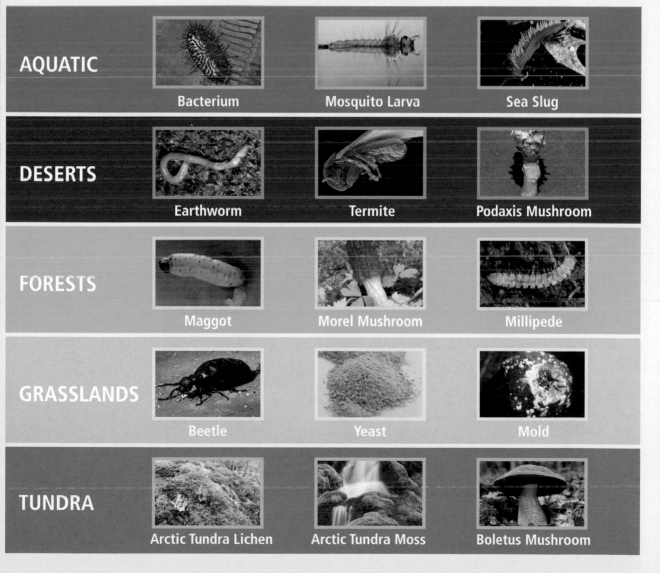

AQUATIC	Bacterium	Mosquito Larva	Sea Slug
DESERTS	Earthworm	Termite	Podaxis Mushroom
FORESTS	Maggot	Morel Mushroom	Millipede
GRASSLANDS	Beetle	Yeast	Mold
TUNDRA	Arctic Tundra Lichen	Arctic Tundra Moss	Boletus Mushroom

Quick Quiz

Based on what you have just read, try to answer the following questions correctly.

1. What is a decomposer?

2. Give an example of a detritivore.

3. What is the umbrella-shaped form of a mushroom?

4. Are decomposers producers or consumers in the food chain?

5. What is detritus?

6. What group of fungi is the deadliest?

7. What do termites mainly eat?

8. Give one example of where bacteria might live.

Answers: 1. A living thing that gets its energy from eating dead plants and animals **2.** Earthworm, maggot, or termite **3.** The fruit of the fungus **4.** Consumers **5.** Dead material that decomposers eat **6.** Fungi from the *amanita* family **7.** Wood **8.** In a body of water or in soil

Glossary

antibiotic: a substance used to hold back the growth of very small living things, including bacteria and fungi

bacteria: one-celled living things too small for the human eye to see

biomes: large areas with the same climate and other natural conditions in which certain kinds of plants and animals live

classified: similar things put together in one group

consumers: animals that feed on plants or other animals

descent: a group of people whose relatives came from the same place

detritus: remains of dead plants and animals

detritus food chain: living things, such as bacteria and earthworms, that work together to break down dead things

energy: the usable power living things receive from food that they use to grow, move, and stay healthy

enzymes: protein that helps decomposition

famine: when there is not enough food to eat and people starve

fungi: living things that make small cells that reproduce instead of seeds

larvae: wormlike babies of insects and some other types of living things

matter: the substances all things are made up of

microscope: an instrument with a lens for making small things look larger

nutrients: substances that provide food for plants and animals

organic: substances that come from plant or animal matter

producers: living things, such as plants, that produce their own food

species: a group of the same kind of living thing; members can breed together

spores: small cells that reproduce; used instead of seeds to make new fungi

Index

Log on to www.av2books.com

AV² by Weigl brings you media enhanced books that support active learning. Go to www.av2books.com, and enter the special code found on page 2 of this book. You will gain access to enriched and enhanced content that supplements and complements this book. Content includes video, audio, web links, quizzes, a slide show, and activities.

Audio
Listen to sections of the book read aloud.

Video
Watch informative video clips.

Embedded Weblinks
Gain additional information for research.

Try This!
Complete activities and hands-on experiments.

WHAT'S ONLINE?

Try This!	Embedded Weblinks	Video	EXTRA FEATURES
Test your knowledge of food chains.	Discover more decomposers.	Watch a video introduction to decomposers.	**Audio** Listen to sections of the book read aloud.
Outline the features of a decomposer.	Learn more about one of the decomposers in this book.	Watch a video about a decomposer.	
Research a decomposer.	Find out more about decomposer conservation.		**Key Words** Study vocabulary, and complete a matching word activity.
Compare decomposers that live in different areas.	Learn more about decomposers.		**Slide Show** View images and captions, and prepare a presentation
Try an interactive activity.			**Quizzes** Test your knowledge.

AV² was built to bridge the gap between print and digital. We encourage you to tell us what you like and what you want to see in the future.

Sign up to be an AV² Ambassador at www.av2books.com/ambassador.

Due to the dynamic nature of the Internet, some of the URLs and activities provided as part of AV² by Weigl may have changed or ceased to exist. AV² by Weigl accepts no responsibility for any such changes. All media enhanced books are regularly monitored to update addresses and sites in a timely manner. Contact AV² by Weigl at 1-866-649-3445 or av2books@weigl.com with any questions, comments, or feedback.